THE OVERTHINKERS DIARY

THE HEART SONG

DR. UPASANA GUPTA

Dedicated to whoever loved, lost, survived, and lived imperfectly

yet beautifully.

Contents

Contents

Contents

Contents

Contents

Contents

You are deleted

"*There were many things i wanted to tell you about,*

But erasing the texts felt more comfortable.

"

Yes the message was deleted, I typed it out, but later realised that

It was not worth sending to you,

The emotions were not worth your time.

It was me, thinking over the things which were insignificant to you.

And yes that's the reason I deleted it, before you could read it

And laugh or ignore the stupid thought of mine.

And, it feels comfortable yet it hurts, to delete it

But you know that's the right thing to do.

Favorite notification

"Once upon a time,

you were my favourite notification"

But now over time, the notification has been turned off,

For better or for worse. Life has moved on.

Now i do not light up with the expectation that

It can be you who has sent me the text or the call.

I do not feed my heart the sweet lies, you once told me

And those which i believed, over and over again.

I have turned all the expectation off.

The night, you & me

"The night speaks about you & me

But the one who listens to it is only me.

"

The night talks about you and me

And the one who hears is only me.

The night whispers about you and me

And the one who loves is only me.

Let's talk

It's easy, how I keep thinking of you

It isn't easy, to how I should be thinking about myself instead.

It's easy to love you.

It isn't easy to let you go.

My choices

"I was proud of my choices

Until i met you

And the choice i made

To choose you, over everything else.. "

Suffocating

"It's suffocating

It's overwhelming

That you know what you are feeling

But still cannot express it at all. "

It's suffocating

How they think

That they know everything about you

And still don't know you at all.

It's suffocating

That you think you know everything about them

And still don't know anything at all.

It's suffocating

How you know everything

And continue to be the same

It's suffocating

How you want to change things

But you cannot change anything at all.

It's suffocating

It's overwhelming

You know what you are feeling

But still cannot express it at all.

Cuts

With every bruise
I radiated bravery
And strength.

I am the diamond
The cuts sparkle.

World of my thoughts

"I am building a world out of my thoughts

Because, the world where i live in

I don't seem to belong here.

"

I am building a whole new world

Out of my mind & out of my thoughts.

Because the world where I live

I no longer belong here

I do not belong to the

People or places.

It's like I am a misfit in a world fitted with perfect people.

So, I am making my own

The one which belongs to me.

Complicated

"You completed me

But, also you complicated me.

"

I wasn't complicated

Until i fell in for you

Chasing a mirage

Looking out for myself

To search for something which I wasn't sure of.

And, though for a while

You completed me

But, also you complicated me.

I love me

"I loved you more

And I loved me less.

But now I love me

And I love me enormously. "

You made me believe that

Love exists, I exist

And that I am important

That's how, you became important than me.

And I loved me less, but loved you more.

But lately I have realised

That was temporary.

I exist and I am important

More than you

My dreams and my self-respect are worth more.

And I need to love me.

More than you or anybody else

So now, I love me

And, I love me enormously

Abundantly

And I will forever.

Hear me

"*Talk about it*

Till they can hear you

And everybody who listens to you

Doesn't necessarily hear you."

Fool

"*If you can fool me*

Believe me Its because I have trusted you a lot.

And from now on I wont be fooled again."

Chase

"*Often we run after them*

Only to find that

We are not being chased.

"

We love them

Those who do not want to be loved.

Only by you

"I wish you could reach me

Whenever I disappear

Because I want to be found but

Only by you"

Can you find me, If i get lost

Or would you just, Let me disappear

From your mind and heart

Can you seek me?

Even if I do not want to be sought

By anybody except you Or would just let me

Evaporate from your memories

Can you love me?

Even when i do not want to be loved

Or would you cherish the absence of me

Can you find me, If I get lost

Because i want to be found

Just by you.

Presence & Absence

"He was unaware of my presence

I was unaware of his absence."

And gradually, neither the presence nor the absence mattered.

Eventually
He didn't matter.
She didn't matter.
They didn't matter.
And life

Life went on.

Under his ink

"I feel beautiful under his ink

And the way he writes me

Pouring all the emotions on the paper

Just to make me as perfect as i can be.

"

I feel beautiful under his ink

The way he writes me with all the love

And how he fills his emotions in the pen

And crafting me stroke by stroke

Making me as perfect as I could be

I feel perfect

Under his ink

Under his love.

Lies

"I laugh at your lies

Because I know the truth

Which you do not want

Your ears to hear."

You know your lies

And I know the truths.

I know you

More than you know yourself.

But for a while I just want to pretend that

You didn't lie and

I was not hurt.

Faces

"Tell me

Which face should i put on today?

Would you like?

The cold one or the happy one"

Tell me which face

Would you want me to put on today

Is It the cold one or the happy one.

The chirpy one or the grumpy one

Or shall I put the one which shows i am strong

Or maybe I can show that i am fragile today.

I have all sets of it

In my cupboard, beside my bed.

And every morning I match it

With the dress I wear

I am still lacking

The mean one

Can you lend me

That mean face of yours

Or the face which you wear

When I need you and your care.

I can face everything

With all faces of mine.

Because, I know what faces you wear

And everybody else.

Permanent

"You lose numerous people in life

And still believe that the

Next person you meet will be "permanent".

"

Thinking game

You wait & wait, over & over again

You think that, they'll think of you.

Or maybe they'll drop you

A "hi" or maybe a wassup

You crave for the need of them

You crave for the attention from them.

It continues, over & over for few days.

Few weeks or maybe few months

You are disappointed

And you take it as it is.

You feel betrayed even though

They never promised you a word.

Neither had they cared, Nor they felt, the way you feel

And maybe you still do.

And, there comes a point when they start fading

From your life, your mind and your contacts

But your heart, it never erases them.

And once in a while or maybe often

When you are alone, You remember them.

And they still don't.

Infinity

"We were bound

To walk together

But on parallel paths

Destined to be together

And meet only at 'infinity'."

Lighthouse

"I will be the lighthouse for you, in the storm

Standing tall, and forever waiting

Just promise, that one day you will come to me."

I will be the lighthouse

For you in the storm

Or whenever it gets dark

Look at me

From wherever you are

I promise to stay tall and forever

For you.

Promise me that

You will come

Looking for me someday.

Rainbow

"*And whenever she lost the colours in her life*

She would sit by the lake and gaze the sky,

And breathe in the rainbow."

Under the summer sky

"I want to weave you in my thoughts

And wrap the warmth around me.

Bcz lately it has been cold

Under the summer sky."

It's cold

In my heart

While waiting for you

In the scorching heat.

Beautiful faces

"*Beautiful faces do not attract me anymore*

Let me know if you have a beautiful soul instead.

"

She is you

"She was the little sunflower

In the farm filled with roses.

"

She was the peace

At the world filled with chaos n drama.

She was the sun of her galaxy

She was love in the world full of lust.

"She is you."

You were the poison

"I was so high on you

That i fell and broke myself.

"

For a while I was drunk on the words you said

And how you made me feel

I was euphoric

Delusional and ecstatic.

And now

It's the deadly hangover

And it aches everywhere.

You were the poison

I drank happily, willingly

And intentionally.

Games

"There are hell lot of games

On play store

And they still choose to

Play with feelings & people.

"

Would you still listen to me?

"Tonight

If I stay quiet

Would you still listen to me?

"

Tonight If I stay alone

Would you just stay beside me?

Tonight If I dream

Would you be in my dreams.

Tonight If I fall asleep

Would you just fall in love with me?

Tonight

Would you?

Forgiveness

"Can I forgive you, they ask me.

Can I forgive myself, I ask me.

"

Beware

The snakes of our lives

The people

Whom we trust

More than ourselves

And they bite us

When we least expect.

Close friends

"They were not that "close" now.

But they were still in each other's

"Close friend" list on instagram.

"

They were not close enough to be friends
But were close on the social media groups

Not close enough to stay together
But close enough to stay connected

Not close enough to talk to each other
But close enough to share meme

They were not close enough to face each other
But were close enough on face-book.

Not close enough
But close enough.

Your name

"Your name was nothing

Till I chose to give it

Meaning and feelings.

"

Exactly like you

"I wish someday you meet somebody

Exactly like you."

Good or bad

That's up to you to decide

Who you are.

Spine-less

"Loving you had made me

Quite spine-less

Let's me un-love you

And zip it up.

"

Loving you indeed had made me spineless

While i forgot

Who I was or what i wanted

I was focussed only on

What you wanted and

Who you were not.

And eventually It made me weak

And i kept getting weaker for the love

You thought i didn't deserve.

But lately i have realised

That loving you wasn't the best

I could do.

So let me Un-love you and Zip up

To brace for, Anything and everything

I desire to get Or to be.

Because I might be flexible

But not spineless

Unspoken words

I can hear you with my eyes,

The unspoken words and unexpressed emotions.

I can listen to you with my eye

And see you through my heart.

And it's okay, if you struggle to tell me

Anything or everything

I know it, when it's wrong or when you are upset.

I can love with all my soul.

You were the best thing

"I'm still in love with you.

But now, I'm not going tell you that

Or admit that

You were the best thing

That had happened to me."

Because you weren't

Rather you were the reason why

Best thing didn't happen to me

Because I chose you

Over the best

And that's why

I was proved wrong.

And though i do not regret

Meeting you

But i wish

I had met someone better

Maybe a little less

Perfect person than you

For an unworthy person like me.

Who knows

I would have been happy

Rather than being

Unhappy with the perfectness.

My enemy

"*Why the night is my enemy*

And not the friend who it used to be.

"

Why the night feels so dear

That i let me be vulnerable

Without any fear

Why does the darkness

Brings out all the wounds

The broken promises

The silent stares

The empty hearts

And the chaotic minds

Why the night makes it vulnerable

To let it go and not to mess it up

The relationship

The love

Or even the life.

Why the night feels so dear

That i let me be vulnerable

Without any fear

Why the night Is my enemy

And not the friend who it used to be.

Pretending

"*And what broke her more wasn't that*

He was happy with them

But it was that

He pretended to be unhappy with her.

"

Lost & found

"I hope

One day

You find peace

Within you

"

I hope

One day

You find yourself

Within you.

Lost & found

you & me.

What can I say

"And what can I say

If you don't want to listen

And how can I love

If you don't want to be loved

And what can I do

If don't want us to happen."

Falling foolishly

"I have been falling

Falling hard For him

And I am sure that

He won't be there

To catch me

Or the falling feelings

"

I have been falling

Falling hard

And falling foolishly.

Two of us

"*It was two of us*

Who started sailing the boat

On the hardships and the depth of life

But to the shore I am content that

You could reach."

It was two of us

On that boat

Sailing over the

Ups & downs of our lives.

But, I am content

That you survived

And that's okay

If I am still

Trying to reach to the shore

Swimming, drowning

And doing everything i can

To meet you there

Once again hoping that

You must be waiting

Waiting for me to survive.

Old photographs

"I still look at the

Old photographs of us

Or even you

And wonder

Will i still take you back?

If you return

Someday"

I still wonder

If you would realise

The havoc you created

And the damage you've done

And would I still take you back

If you return

But, will you Return?

Stranger

There is always a

Familiar stranger

In everybody's life

Whom we knew

But now we question

If we actually knew.

Maybe in may

"Maybe in May,

You will be mine

And I'll be yours."

Maybe in May

You will show the love

Your harbour

And may be in May

It would be little less painful

Than it is now

May be in May

It won't be a maybe

And I will be sure

That you are going to stay

Maybe in May.

If fingers could speak

"If fingers could speak,

They would have told you about

The numerous times

When i wrote your name

On the piece of paper,

Caressed and erased again. "

I have written your name Over and over again

On the paper And on my heart.

Ask the papers Or the ink

Or the heart that beats

For you.

Your name is my favourite.

I want to color you

I want to

Color you red green purple and pink

Blue black and little of yellow

Till you've got

All shades of me.

I want to color you

With the color of my soul

The darkest desires

And with the innocent wishes.

I want to put

The darkest color

So that you cannot wipe me away from your heart.

I want to color you

With the color of me.

Let me do that.
Please.

Saviour

"*He is saving himself from the pain*

She causes when he loves her

By only loving her

When he needs it

And not when she wants it."

And she is saving him from getting hurt

By not causing pain And letting him do

Whatever he wants, Whenever he wants

However he wants

Even if it, Rips her heart.

Conditionally

"He loves her, conditionally

Whenever he wants & however he wants.

And she lets him do it, unconditionally

Whenever he wants & however he wants."

Love with *terms and conditions attached. `

Is it love or mutual fund investment?

I want to hold a hand

"In the world

Where everybody is counting

The number of kisses they've had till now

I still want to hold a hand

For as long as i can"

I want to hold your hand

And never let it go

And feel the crisp line

Or the soft knuckles.

I want to feel

The things which you don't want to say

But the fingers say it all.

I want to get those Goosebumps

When you touch your palm against mine

And hook it in.

I know how you don't want to express your love

But the way you hold my hand

Says it all.

It's has everything

Passion, love, sense of security

When i hold your hand.

It's like

I have the world

In my palms.

And i don't care about the rest.

You & me

"I loved you &

You loved yourself too."

And amidst that
i was left unloved.

Existence

"*On the sleepless nights & the restless days*

I have always wondered how you stay calm

And pretend that I do not exist

In this world. "

And I pretend to not know this

While doing the best I can to smile

And eventually end up failing in both.

The pretend game sucks.

You pretend and pretend and pretend

that you are okay.

Eventually ending up

Exhausted to love

Or to live.

Am I important

"One day he told i was important

And the other day he showed i wasn't

I am still unable to decide

Which day i to believe in."

And if i was important

Why did your actions told

The opposite of your words

And if you cared

Why did you choose to stay quiet?

And let me go

And if you loved

Why did you only say?

And not chose to show

And if i was misunderstanding

Why did you not understand?

And explain.

And if i was hurting

Why did it not hurt you?

To see me in pain.

Why.

Cure

"*Love is the cure for the pain*

Love gives.

"

When you left

"*The heart misses you badly*

But the mind still remembers

And is hurt over the words you used

When you left.

"

Stranger

"I wish I could tell you that

I am afraid to lose you

"

I am afraid to be a stranger

When I know everything about you and

You know all about me.

I am afraid to pass by

Without noticing you

When I can see you coming

From miles away.

I wish I could tell you

I still think of you and about us

When all I show that

I don't care at all.

I wish I could pretend

Nothing happened between us

When all I remember are the moments we lived together.

I wish I could tell you

That there is an emptiness

All around and within me.

I'm in love with you

"*I'm in love with you*

Whether I'm with you

Or without you.

"

I was in love

Even before I knew I was

Even when you were not around

And even when you didn't know.

And for me loving you is a feeling with which

I've decided to live for the rest of my life

With the subconscious love

Somewhere breathing inside me

I know that

I am in love with you

Because I'm in love with you

Whether you are with me

Or without me

Irrespective of the expectation

Or desire to be loved by you.

I want to forget you

"*I will write you in poems*

And lose you in my stories

That's the way

I want to forget you.

"

A thousand times

"I can love you

A thousand times,

Even if you agree

To love me just once

"

I can die

A thousand times

Even if you promise to

Live for me

Just once.

Without any reason

"*I had every reason*

Not to fall far you

But then

Love happens

Without any reason."

Crazily & unintentionally

"*And they loved*

Without letting others know

And without even letting

Each other know

That there were in love

Crazily & unintentionally."

And if I was important

"*And if I was important*

Why the actions did told the opposite of your words."

And if I was important

Why did your actions tell

The opposite of your words

And if you cared

Why did you choose to stay quiet

And let me go

And if you loved

Why did you only say

And not choose to show

And if I was misunderstanding

Why did you not understand and explain?

And if I was hurting

Why did it not hurt you

To see me in pain.

Why.

I was broken

I was broken by the expectations

I had with myself that I would be

Loved without

Any conditions attached.

But now I've healed.

And put some more gold

At the broken edges Of my unloved heart.

It would be different

"Why do you weep my heart?

Did you really think?

It would be different

This time."

I Love You

"There are various ways

By which I show that

I love you

And sometimes it's just by

Staying quiet, hiding my emotions

From the world & you."

There are various ways by which I show that

I love you and sometimes

It's just by staying quiet,

Hiding my emotions

And shedding a tear or two.

Letting myself understand the fact that

Loving you doesn't mean that

You must love me back

Or I should be your priority.

Loving you is an emotion

An engraving over my heart

Like the tattoo i have on my wrist

It will forever be there

Till I live.

Loving you doesn't mean

I must have you by my side

All the time, all the moments

It's an emotion

Which i can choose

To show or not to show

But it stays

Forever inside me.

Paint it into poetry

Hurt me with your actions

And I'll choose not to react

But to bleed through my words

On a piece of paper

And will create a masterpiece

Called poetry.

And that's how I'd choose to

Fight and survive

And if you think that makes me

Weak or coward

I pity your inconclusive mind

Bcz that's what I think

Strength is.

Undo

"I can undo loving you

Only if i undo living

And that doesn't mean

I need to live with you

I'm just in love with you."

Plethora of emotions

"To the plethora of emotions

I feel when you brush

Your little finger with mine

The sun sets over my cheeks

As your eyes tease my smile.

"

And then

While I shy away

You hold me close to your heart

and life.

And this is what

Romance to me is.

I love the way you love me

"I love the way you love me

As you were reading a manual on how i must be loved.

"

I love the way

You love me

As you were reading a manual

On how I must be loved

And cared with affection and care.

I love the way

You look at me

As you have always known

How I want to be glanced

Like the way we gaze at the stars.

I love the way

You hold me

As if you have always desired to

Hold me closer and know

How fragile I was to hold.

I love the way you love me.

As if you've always been

In love with my soul and as if we were

The soul mates from the old galaxies.

Wipe it

"*I want to wipe the doubt*

I have on my mind

That you need me

When you clearly do not."

I want to make the state clear again

Because maybe it was something

You didn't want to write

And wrote accidentally.

I wish I could wipe you off

From my heart

And the moist traces you left

Over my face

I want to wipe you off

From my skin

And your gentle touch

On my soul.

I want to make the slate clear again

Maybe it was something

You didn't want to write

And wrote accidentally.

I want to wipe all of it.

Bring me love &

I'll give you a home to stay.

Bring me care
and I'll give you a heart to reside in.

Bring me you
and I'll give a life to live in.

Read me

"Read me in between the lines of your book

I'm hidden amidst the paragraphs

And you can often find me before the full stop."

Read me in between the lines

Of your favourite book.

I'm found amidst the paragraph

And often before the full stop.

Read me the way you read

Each word and every letter.

I can sometimes be silent

And often spelled out loud.

Sometimes I'm heart wrenching

And sometimes I'm the erotica.

Sometimes you'll find me to be a mystery

While often I've been written over

A period of times as classics.

I'm the verb, adjective and the noun

I can often be the exclamation

And sometimes I'm hidden in the

Semicolons and commas.

Read me as you reach everything

With interest and affection.

Read me

Till your last breath

And read every inch of my skin.

It doesnt hurt

"It doesn't hurt now

Neither your words nor

Your absence
"

It doesn't hurt now

Neither my eyes

Nor my heart.

They don't hurt now

Neither the people

Nor the situations'

It doesn't hurt now

Neither the life

Nor the death

Maybe.

What hurts now is

The hope

The unexpected love

Or happiness's.

I wish i could

"I wish i could read minds and hearts

Because what my heart listens

And mind says when you talk is entirely opposite."

You speak your heart through your mind

And I speak my mind through my heart.

I wish I could understand

Whether you are true to your heart

Or it's the mind controlling you.

I tried reading your eyes,

But have been often misled

By my own perceptions of you.

So, I wish I could read mind & hearts

Before I sin to fall for you again.

All over again

"*Just when i thought*

Everything was over,

You smiled

& my hopes lit

All over again."

Too tired to play

"And sometimes she was too tired to play

That she let go every shot thrown at her

In spite of knowing that she could win

If she played with all her heart."

And sometimes, she was too tired to play

Too tired to pick her weapons and fight

That she let go every shot thrown at her.

In spite of knowing that

She could win

If she played with all her heart

And her mind.

She knew that she was the best

But she was exhausted,

And injured of carrying the emotions and

Expectations.

So, she decided to play dumb for a while

To duck for all the shots, thrown at her.

For a while she let it go,

And did not play.

Till she was ready to play all over again

The one you need

"I may never be the one you want

But i will always be the one you need."

I may never be the one you want.

But I will always be the one you need.

I may never be the one you desire

but I will always be the one on whom you can lean.

I may never be the one whom you wait for

but I will always be the one to wait for yo

For a while

"For a while,

Let me just wrap myself up and hide

From the expectations and you."

For a while,

Let me just wrap myself up and hide

From the expectations and you.

Let me hide myself

So that you cannot find me

And neither the disappointments.

Let's forget and forgive each other

"Let's forget and forgive each other

For the things we did and

For the things we didn't

And let's accept that

Something's are not meant to be together

For better."

Let's forget and forgive each other

For the things we did and

For the things we didn't.

And let's accept that

Something's are not meant to be together.

For better.

Let's, forgive forget n accept

Let's accept that we were too naive to understand

Each other or the situation.

Sometimes things aren't meant to be

And they are just meant to meet

And leave.

For better, for the worse

To let us grow.

Burning

He was burning me at his fingertip

While i thought that he was holding me.

And after a while,

Though i could smell the fumes

And see the ashes out of my soul

But, i was addicted to the "flames"

To the extent that

I couldn't feel the pain,

And believed that i deserved it.

Until i realised that,

I should be burning my own fire

Rather than burning in someone else's.

Complementary yet incomplete

"I might never be enough for you

And you'll always be sufficient for me."

I might never be good for you

And you'll always be best for me

I might never be the reality for you

And you'll always be a dream for me.

You & me

Complementary yet incomplete.

You & me

Together yet Apart.

In the crowd

"Sometimes,

It's just that one person

Visible to you in the crowd

And you can see nothing else.

"

Walk with me

Talk to me

Like the wind does

And I would tell you

How you've always made me feel.

Because,

I might not always say

What you mean to me

Or how you make me feel

The butterfly in my stomach

Or the racing heartbeat

The sweaty palm

And the glistening eyes.

It's what you make me feel

And that's what

Love to me is.

Real n Reel

"*You are the "reel"*

I shall be "real" instead.

You be the trend

I shall be a "friend" instead.

You be the temporary

I shall be "everlasting" instead."

Believe you

"*And i choose to believe you again and again*

Not because i don't know that

You cannot be trusted

But because i still believe that

You can change."

Stupid

"That's the "beauty of love"

We fall for stupid things

Stupid people

At some

Stupid situation "

We fall for stupid people

At stupid circumstances

And stupid times

For all the stupid reasons.

Looking for love

"You are looking for love.

All around you

I was looking for you,

All around me "

You look for love

I look for you.

Because for me

It's the same.

You were my priority

“*You were my priority*

And now, you are not even a necessity.
”

Written by you

"*I desire to be written by you,*

Because on those crumpled papers

May be you'll fall in love with me

Again. "

I desire to be written by you.

Will you write me

In your words?

I desire to be written by you.

Will you write me

With your love?

I desire to be written by you.

Will you write me

And let me stay

Forever in your heart.

Words

"*Words, it's not everything.*

You can hear with your eyes

And listen with your heart.

"

Bcz, words can be misleading.

The letters can be false

The sentences can be wrongly framed

But the feelings,

Hear them instead.

They met, again & again

"*They met, again & again*

Even when they had already said their good-byes."

And each time, they lived like an eternity,

In those moments of staying together.

They knew they had to part ways.

So, whenever they met, it was surreal.

They made memories,

Without a single picture together.

And they wondered,

Is this how soul mates are supposed to be?

To a world

"Take me to a world where you exist

Take me to a world where i exist

Take me to a world where we exist

Take me to a world where nobody else exists

Take me to a world where love exists."

She was his poetry

"

She was his poetry which he weaved in his flute,

Every day

And he was the music which she wrote in her poems,

Every night "

Our scars

"We hide our scars, under the skin and the clothes,

And sometimes, we hide it beneath our soul,

Because we are afraid,

About getting judged or identified by that piece of wound.

"

Will you still love me

"Will you still love me

If I showed you my scars

Or will you just abandon me

If I am not as good as you are

"

Will you still care

If I showed where it hurts

Or will you judge me

If I am made up of defective parts.

Will you still believe me

If I showed you my truth

Or will you just feed me lies

And disown me somehow.

Will you love me?

The sweet lies

"*Stop feeding me the sweet lies*

Woven in your words

"

I can see the truth

Scattered around me

But still, decide to overlook them

Bcz, I am scared to let you go

For now.

For now,

I cannot let you go.

But the future is unseen.

Insignificant

"Some days i desire to talk to you

I type the text and erase it

Over and over again.

Bcz suddenly i remember

How "insignificant" I'm to you.

"

I obsess over the days

When it was easier to communicate with you

Everything was simple

We could talk for hours

Or maybe it was me

Thinking that and feeling that.

And, some days i still desire

To talk to you like the older days

I dial your number but disconnect before it rings

I type the text and erase it,

Over and over again.

Bcz suddenly i remember

How "insignificant" I'm to you.

And how you are so

"full of yourself"

Belong to you

"It hurts to see you

Not mine.

When all my thoughts

Belong to you. "

It's hurtful

To see you not mine

When all of my thoughts

Belong to you.

It's hurtful

To see you love

Somebody else

When all I can do is

To love you.

April 1

"They love fooling you,

While, you are the fool in love

"

Yes, i was fooled by you, again

Yet i believed you, again

You laughed at me, again

And I regretted believing you, again

Doesnt matter whether it was

April 1st or December 31st,

You love fooling me,

And I'm the

Fool in love.

Careless

"There are numerous people who love us

Yet, We still care about the one

Who doesn't"

Let me hand over your heart back

Today I have finally decided,

To hand over your heart back.

No, it's not because I do not love you.

But, it's because I love myself a little more.

I need my peace, my mental wellness,

I want to let go of my insecurities, my fear, my inferiority complex,

That was only because I love you,

A little more.

Your love is way too costly,

And I prefer not to buy it.

I am saving the pieces of me for myself,

For now.

So, let me hand over your heart back.

And let go of the toxicities.

No matter if I am alone,

But that doesn't make me lonely now.

I am enough for myself.

Evil side of my heart

"There's this evil side of my heart

Wanting to break your heart as you break mine

But, then you smile and the good side takes over."

There's this evil side of my heart,

The real dark one,

Who hates you for ignoring me or my messages,

Wanting to break your heart as you break mine

Ruthlessly.

But, then you smile

And the good side takes over

The silly one, the naive

The innocent one

In love with you, hopelessly.

Endlessly.

Hold me

"Hold me

Before we fall"

Hold me

Before we give up.

Hold me

Before we let it go.

Hold me

Till the feelings return

Hold me

Till we fall in love

Again.

Let's pretend, about you & me

"*Let's pretend, you exist*

Let's pretend, about you & me."

Let's pretend, you exist

Let's pretend, we are strangers

Let's pretend, we ever met

Let's pretend, you ever smiled

Let's pretend, you ever cared

Let's pretend, we ever had a good time.

Let's pretend, you meant anything

Let's pretend, we ever loved

Let's pretend, about it all

Let's pretend, about you & me.

Wrong time

"*And at the end, she knew he was the right one,*

But it was the wrong time."

A pile of ash

"You burn yourself in the name of love

And when it's the actual time to ignite yourself,

You've already been a pile of ash."

We burn yourself in the name of love

Sometimes, out of stupidity

And sometimes, for the sake of fantasies

And we carry the pain of the burnt heart in you

Silently, showing off as if nothing has ever happened

We smile, you laugh, while deep down

It's still burning

In the guilt, or the regret.

Over years, the flame settles down

And sometimes we even forget

But, by the time we feel the spark again

We cannot ignite it

Why.

Bcz, its all ashes left

Inside of you.

Its ashes, scars,

With nothing left over.

Story

"*You keep checking your story*

Till that one person has viewed it."

Propose me

"Propose me, with some unspoken word

Lemme hear your love, in the words unheard."

Propose me

With that love in your eyes

I don't ask for

Shiny ring or the wine.

Propose me

With the warmth of your heart

I don't want that

Fancy limousine or the cart.

Propose me

When you want me for a lifetime

I don't mind waiting

An eternity for that time

Propose me

Even if you've nothing to offer

I don't care

If i had to hold on to you forever.

Propose me

With some unspoken word

Lemme hear

Your love in the words unheard.

Show it

"*Love, if you can't say it*

You have to show it

If you can't show it,

You have to say it."

Hold on

"Hold on

Let me heal

Before you hurt me

Again."

Hold on

Let me heal

Before you hurt me

Again.

Hold on

Let me live

Before you ask me

To love again.

Would you remember my name?

If one day, I ask you

What were you most afraid to lose

Would you remember my name?

If one day, I ask you

What were you most afraid to love

Would you remember my name?

If one day, I ask you

What were you most afraid to let go

Would you remember my name?

If one day, I ask you

Who taught you to love and live

Would you remember my name?

And, if one day, I ask you

Who am I & what's my name

Will you still remember the name?

Unseen Untouched

He kissed her with his eyes

Like the way he always did

Not all the love

Has to be expressed with touch

Some can be unseen, untouched

Yet immensely loved.

Flaws

They looked at everything
and every flaw she had.
They ripped her out of her emotions.

And the only thing they failed to notice was
who she was and how she was drowning
in her skin and in her own life.
And there was no one
to rescue her.

Apocalypse

"*We were two worlds*

different yet complementary

inhabiting one soul

but in different time zones.

"

We revolved together

in the universe on parallel paths.

We wished we would meet someday.

But, that would be an apocalypse.

Wounds on the back

"the wounds on the back

are loved more than are hated"

The wounds on the back hurt
More than on the heart.

The wounds on the back
heal slower than of the heart.

The wounds on the back
are hard to see.

The wounds on the back
are harder to believe.

The flower you loved

"the flower you loved

blooms in my heart.

"

The flowers you loved

I have planted them in my heart

they grow through my veins

as my love waters them

they bloom like your smile.

I surround myself with the

fragrances of the petals

they remind me

those days when

we were together.

Private possession

"He saved her from the world

and kept her as his private possession"

He loved her insanely and protected her

from the indecent and evil world.

He created a world around her where she could have

everything she wanted

except for the freedom.

On repeat

I was your favourite song

you played me over and over again, on repeat mode.

And now when you are done

you have paused me and skipped my presence.

And here I am

waiting you to un-pause me to play my life

even if you don't want to hear it any more.

I wish I could play another song

which never reminded me of you.

Let me love you

"Let me love you, one last time

Coz, tomorrow onwards

I'll love myself."

Let me love you, one last time

Let me touch you, one last time

Let me hear you, one last time

Let me feel you, one last time

Let me pamper you, one last time.

Let me hold you, one last time

Let me kiss you, one last time.

Because, tomorrow onwards

I will love myself, hold myself, feel myself, live myself

And be proud of myself.

I want to paint me and you

I want to paint myself with the colour that attracts you.

I want to paint me with the colour that makes you

see me the way I see you.

I want to paint me with every colour

maybe then you will fancy me

I want to paint me with the colour of

you and your love.

I want to paint me and you in to one colour

and make a whole new shade.

You are the favourite piece of my puzzle

You are like the prettiest messiest piece of my puzzle.

I try to mould you adjust you, solve you.

I wonder, are you even a part of my puzzle

or you are just lost piece of someone else's puzzle.

But, no matter what or whether you will ever fit in or not

You'll always be my favourite part of my puzzle.

Can I love you

*"Can I keep you by my side tonight
and not just into my phone?"*

Can I hold you tonight and not just hold my phone

Can I talk to you in person looking into your eyes

and not just the screen?

Can I hear you laugh and feel your whisper

and not just the voice?

Can I love you and watch you sleep tonight

and not just dream about you like every other night.

Can I keep you by my side tonight

as I keep the phone at my side?

A mess

"I wanted to be your art

But, you sketched me into a mess."

I wanted to be everything you wanted to draw

i wanted to be everything you paint

I wished to be your muse

I wished to be your art.

But you sketched me into a mess.

A mess that is impossible to be re-drawn

Or painted again.

You are the sun

"*When it's time*

You have to stop

Revolving around them

And be your own sun.

"

Temporary

"She was looking for something

But, that wasn't me

I was a transit for her temporary halt."